Steps To Hiring Exceptional Hospitality Property Staff

Hotels-Resorts-Inns-Bed and Breakfasts-Vacation Homes

By

Gerry MacPherson
Keystone Hospitality Property Development

Table of Contents

1. The Right Mindset

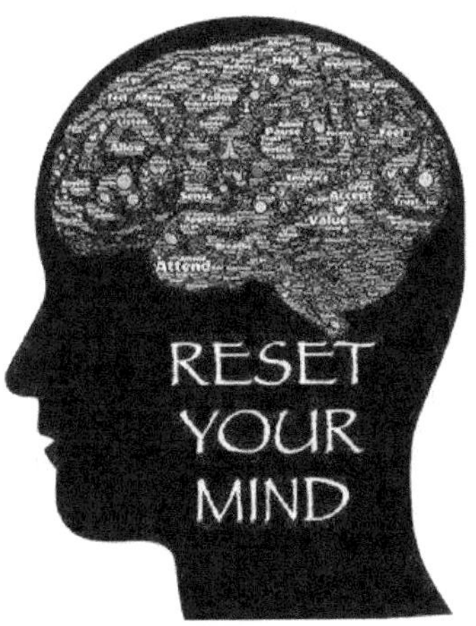

The past number of years has been an interesting study of hospitality property owners in way of thinking. Many have had a negative mindset due to the dramatic change in the economy and the hospitality property service culture.

So, let's look at the downturn of the economy as an example of how we can change our mindset and that of our employees.

After the economy started to fall more than a few hospitality properties failed because they did not keep up with the changes. Low occupancy rates caused belt-tightening to save money and often one of the first effects was employee cutbacks. This was understandable, but quite often the staff that remained had to take on added duties, sometimes duties they were unprepared for.

I had seen in many cases, where hotel management did not take the time to retrain the remaining staff. This caused a great deal of stress. When your staff are not properly trained, overworked and stressed, it does not take long for your services to slide.

When employees have extra duties and little time, the idea of taking additional time to train does not seem feasible but any property wishing to remain competitive and successful has to make training a top priority.

The clientcle numbers you are attracting might not be as high as you want or need, but the guests who do utilize your property, expect good service. This is where management has to take the time to re-interview the staff and determine their strengths and weaknesses.

In times of economic slowdowns, you might have seen your staff taking on duties they had done when they first started. Making this kind of change without proper communication could lead to disgruntled employees. This is where it is very important to hold a staff meeting and explain the situation. You explain that times are tough but your goal is to keep your property open and the remaining staff employed. Most often, employees will be happy they still have a job.

It is at this time you have to enforce the importance of teamwork and I don't just mean the front line employees. It means everybody from the owner down.

If employees see the owner and management pulling together in all aspects of operating the property, more often than not, a sense of loyalty will shine through and you'll see everyone putting forth a little extra effort to help the business keep going through the tough times. If you continue to be honest with your employees, sharing how you see the future, it'll often give them a clear mindset and the desire to help the business through the rough times.

It is at times like this, being supportive of your staff is imperative. Some things to consider:

- *If staff have extra duties, don't be a stickler to an exact time schedule.*
- *Give them the freedom to make decisions when it comes to customer service and back their decisions.*
- *Remain positive*

As the owner, you will be your employee's source of inspiration and the best way to show inspiration is by your work habits.

The work you do and the way you do what it is a reflection of who you are.

- *If disorderly at your work, it's because you're disorderly inside.*
- *If you're always late, it's because you are late inside.*
- *If you are jaded with your work, it's because you are jaded inside.*
  "If you're not the role model you wish your employees to follow, how could you start changing your mindset?"

What aspects of your life would you like to improve? Let's look at some possibilities.

- *Do you procrastinate?*
- *Do you fail to follow through?*
- *Are you loud and inpatient?*
- *Do you feel overwhelmed?*

Many of these traits could be the cause root of drudgery. Often drudgery is not the result of a poor business concept or lack of planning, it might mean you do not have the right strategic mindset. Planning and developing activities is imperative to your business's success: forecasting, budgeting, projecting sales and revenue, staff planning are all important to meet your business commitments. But they do not mean your business will prosper.

"You have to be in the right mindset, a strategic mindset." The word *"strategy"* makes many people nervous. I've had many owners tell me when they think of business strategy, they think of countless hours working on details, loads of research and numerous meetings. Developing a strategic mindset does not require all that. You can take an hour today to start and then embrace it over time.

We have all heard that it's important to live in the moment and in certain situations that is true. That is not helpful when thinking of your business. For your business to be successful you have to have a vision.

What is your business going to be like next year, in five years, in 10 years?

You must have broader goals and any day-to-day decisions should relate to both your immediate business and your long-term goals.

Let me say that again, a strategic mindset gets you thinking about how your business decisions today will impact your business in the future. Thinking daily about your strategic mindset, allows you to grow and change logically. You don't intend to reach a strategic goal today but instead, get a step closer to it.

1.1 Here is where you start

Use these 6 steps to establish a strategic mindset for your business planning and tasks. Spend only 10 minutes on each step *(it is a good idea to do the first two steps together)*. Repeat the process once or twice a month and you will rapidly get beyond urgency and into a strategic way of thinking.

1.2 The 6 steps to a strategic mindset

Step 1: What Do I Want My Business to Become?

As I said, don't spend a lot of time on these exercises, take 10 minutes or less and write down a 1- to 2 sentence answer to this question. Be specific, but not detailed; for example, you might want to become the hospitality property of choice in your region. You don't have to think of the details such as marketing budget, revenue targets and room design. Instead, describe your target market and why they should choose your property to stay.

If you like, you can share this answer with friends and/or colleagues. Watch their reactions, listen to their ideas or suggestions and adjust your answers to echo the best ideas. It is important to use your wisdom here, you don't have to include everyone's ideas or suggestions. Once you're happy with your answers, you now have a goal, you have a vision statement, a vision you can work towards. You must check in regularly.

Step 2: What is My Business?

In 10 minutes or less write down what your business is and does. Again, in a short paragraph, consider these topics when answering.

- *Who is your clientele?*
- *What services or products will you provide?*
- *Are you going to stay at your current location or are you going to expand?*
- *What makes you distinctive from your competitors?*
- *What are your values or philosophy, both business and personal?*
- *What is your commitment to the use of new technology?*

This brief paragraph is your map to reaching your vision: the vision is now your mission statement. It will help you focus on how you plan to achieve that vision *(big picture)*.

Again, share this statement with your friends and colleagues, and watch their reactions, listen to their ideas or suggestions and using your wisdom to adjust your answers. When you feel comfortable with your statement, you have to consider it on a day-to-day basis. When considering changes or adjustments in your business, your mission statement helps you know when to say *"yes"* and when to say *"no"*.

Step 3: Set a Goal

Give yourself a couple of minutes of quiet time, close your eyes and visualize your business as it will be in the future:

- *How did you get there?*
- *What steps did you have to take to achieve that vision?*
- *What kind of research and planning did it require?*
- *Will you have to make any changes to reach your goal?*

Try to be exact when thinking of your vision.

These questions will help you outline the path required to reach your vision. In a few moments, you should have an idea of your goal and the basic ideas of how you are going to make it happen. If you like, you can again ask for input.

Step 4: Implement Your Goal

This might sound a little fast from going from a vision to action, but it's important to prove your visions can succeed. Select one of your ideas, one of your goals and start to implement it. Decide what you need to accomplish this task, decide who you are going to need or what vendor is required to help and discuss the possibilities. If your vision is clear, don't let anyone's initial *"no"* discourage you.

You are now taking the first steps to action, planting the seeds in other minds, and setting the steps toward your goal.

Step 5: Gage and Evaluate Your Progress
What do you have to do to implement your goal?
It is important to stay on top of each step.

Gage and evaluate your progress.

You can measure your progress by communicating with others, reviewing any relative data, and it's okay to go with your gut. Don't spend a lot of time evaluating each step, just a couple of minutes will do.

Remember, you're taking small steps to support something larger. Taking a couple of minutes to measure in the beginning allows you to test your footing.

Step 6: Revisit

If you have taken only the allocated 10 minutes to do each of the five phases, then in less than an hour you have created a vision and mission, set a strategic goal that supports the statement, acted on it and measured your action.

That is very impressive!

So, is that it?

Do you have the right strategic mindset?

Not just yet.

This is an exercise to a way of thinking about your business, a way of seeing and doing that you carry into your daily work.

Okay, take 10 minutes to review what you've done and answer the following questions.

- *Do your vision and mission still ring true?*
- *In developing a strategic goal to support those statements, did you identify potential improvements to your vision and mission?*

- *Can you realistically act in a step-by-step fashion toward your goal?*
- *Can you measure that action and its progress?*

Make any adjustments that you would deem necessary.

Once you're happy with all the steps, you can use them as a template to help you to form a habit of tackling your business's future with each activity you engage in. I realize that some strategy sessions will take longer than the one-hour exercise you have done here, however, by using these steps a few times and becoming comfortable with the process, it will be of incredible benefit when it comes to major strategizing for your business.

1.3 Does this activity have real value?

If you have a clear vision of who you are and what your business is, as well as the steps you need to take to achieve your goals, you will not be dragged down into the pool of drudgery but instead, you will be an inspiration to both your employees and customers. A clear and strategic mindset will enable you to keep your head up, take new actions and move your business forward. By making these changes a permanent and formal part of your operation, your business will grow as you take great strides toward reaching your vision.

So you might ask *"How can I use this mindset strategy to demonstrate the importance of even the most menial tasks in our day-to-day operation?"*

Share with your employees the different steps and how they work to achieve the goal. Show them how even the most menial work can be a piece of art when done by an artist. Show them how they can look at each job, each task as one with a goal, and by reaching this goal gain a sense of pride.

Every job, every task, is important to the vision of your property and every employee's contribution is important to reaching your goals. There is no such thing as undesirable work, but there could be employees who see certain kinds of work as undesirable. By relaying the importance of every job and allowing your staff to shine, they will stop looking at their work as punishment but instead as an opportunity to see themselves as they are.

Now it's time to start working on your goals.

2. How To Hire Winners

I have seen hospitality property owners go from one extreme to another when it comes to their hiring process. One property owner might take the time to study the candidate and ask thoughtful questions while another might look like a new person and say, *"Do know how to use a computer? Okay, you are hired."* For it to work, the interview process has to be consistent. It has to be scripted the same way every time.

As in all other tasks in your hospitality property, your hiring process should be documented in your operations manual.

When looking for new employees, before doing anything else, talk to business associates, colleagues and competitors. You might find that a little strange but if you have a good working relationship with your competition, they could be a great source of information.

2.1 What is the next step?

1. When there is a position open and you have several candidates interested, the first thing you should do is hold a group meeting with all the candidates. At the meeting, you give a scripted presentation describing your business's history and successes as a hospitality property. You describe how your property works with an operation manual and that all employees have to agree to work within these guidelines. Then you describe the attributes you would require a successful candidate to have for the position. *(Many times at this point, candidates will disqualify themselves from the process.)*

2. You make arrangements and meet with candidates individually. You discuss their reactions and feelings to the group meeting.

It is at this time I should tell you, we here at Keystone HPD believe that since we're in the hospitality property industry, customer service is of vital importance. It is our feeling that every position does not always have to be filled by someone with years of experience or a graduate degree.

The kind of candidate we would look for is someone with compassion.

Compassion cannot be taught. A property with compassionate employees, who can think and feel like your customers, will go a lot further with gaining customer loyalty than a property with employees that lack compassion. If your property is working with an operations manual and every job is described on a step-by-step basis, then most jobs can be taught.

With that in mind, some interview questions might differ a bit from what you're used to. Here are samples of the type of interview questions you could ask. For example:

Where have you been employed in the past and what did you learn from those experiences?
This is a very basic question, but with it, you can start to get an idea of a person's background and strengths and weaknesses.

How long were you employed in your previous position?
Here you are looking for commitment and loyalty and it's okay to ask why they left your last job.

Why would you like to take your position?
Such questioning can reveal details about the candidate's enthusiasm for the job.

Why do you feel you're suitable for this position?
Suitability can be defined as the candidate being able to fit into the business and position that the candidate intends to fill.

What do you have that other candidates don't?
Like a property, your goal is to distinguish yourself from your competitors, so it is fair to ask the same of your employees.

You can evaluate the candidate on the technical skills, behavioural skills and ability to build strong customer relationships.

I've heard many employers ask potential candidates *"What are your strengths?"*

To me, this has never been a great question.

It is at this point I would ask for a PAR story. A PAR story is where the candidate describes a problem they have encountered, the action taken and the result. Ask about handling a customer complaint; an emergency; a problem while working with a team.

Let them talk!

It is an open-ended question where you can gauge the candidate's ability to react quickly on their feet, and again, their strengths and weaknesses.

What accomplishment are you most proud of personally, as a team member?

Here you can get an idea of their priorities and how they would work with a group.

What would you do if you found your co-worker stealing, doing any wrong activities or spreading rumours?

In the hospitality property industry, honesty is very important because guests have to trust that a property worker who enters their room will not steal their personal belongings. You have to have policies in place for this type of situation.

You want to keep the interview as positive and as relaxed as possible, but sometimes the position you are hiring for could be stressful.

Here are a few stress questions you could ask to see how the candidate reacts.

What would you say if I told you this interview was going badly?

Why haven't you progressed more in your career?
Is that the best answer you can give me? Let's move on.

They may sound a little harsh, but they are nothing compared to angry customers yelling at them because the rooms are not ready.

Why do you want to work with our property and what are your goals in the future?

With this question, you can best judge the candidate on their expectations from this job and if their plans involve working with your property.

In general, I do not feel it is appropriate to ask about a person's age, gender, sexual preference, religion, family planning or political leanings when it comes to hiring at a hospitality property. In some countries these questions are illegal.

Before making any decisions, ask the candidates how they feel about the following statements.

"The customer is not always right, but whether they are or not, it is our job to make them feel that way."

"Everyone who works here is expected to work toward being the best they can be at the tasks they are accountable for. If they are unwilling, they should leave."

"The business is a place where everything we know how to do is tested by what we don't know how to do and that the conflict between the two is what creates growth, and that creates meaning."

Their responses can give you another indication of whether the candidates are right for your property.

After you have made your decision…

> 3. If you have not done so in person, notify the successful candidate by telephone. Again, use a scripted presentation.

> 4. Notify the unsuccessful candidate, thanking each for their interest. A standard letter, signed by the interviewer. This goes a long way into showing the professionalism of your property.

> 5. The first day of training with the new employee should start with the owner, and include the following:

- *A sit-down with the owner to review the property's organizational structure and vision.*
- *Summarizing the system explaining how it works in the day-to-day operation*
- *Taking a tour of the facilities, highlighting people at work, and show the systems at work to demonstrate the interdependence of the systems on people and the people on systems.*
- *Answer all questions clearly and fully*
- *Issue the employee their uniform and operations manual*
- *Review the operations manual and have the employees sign a form indicating they understand the concept and have received the manual.*

- *Complete the employee paperwork*

For some of you, this might seem a little much, for others, it's totally clear, either way, the step-by-step process, if done consistently works and your reward — incredible, loyal employees.

Make these tactics part of your ongoing operation strategy and you'll find the quality and consistency of your employees rise dramatically.

3. Can't Afford Employee Training Programs? Think Again

Let me ask you something.

"Do you have a small property, just a couple of employees but you seem to be doing most of the work?"
or
"Do you have a property running on a shoestring budget, with limited employees that are overworked?"
or
"Are you so busy that you cannot find the time to think about additional training for your employees?"
or
"Do you have high turnover?"

If you have answered *"yes"* to any of these questions, there is no doubt in my mind you're leaving money on the table and over the years have probably lost some excellent employees.

I have not talked to many hospitality property owners who said: *"I'm very happy if my business is so-so."*

Most owners want their properties to be successful. Being organized is a great start but a sure-fire way to help your business grow is to train your employees and I don't mean just when they are hired, it has to be ongoing.

You might be thinking about these questions.

- *"Why would I want to take on the extra expense?"*
- *"When are we going to find the time?"*
- *"And if I train my employees, won't they leave for better opportunities?"*

Training can improve employee morale, business performance, help increase your profits and if you have a properly organized system, you can find the time.

Let's dig into this a little further. Here are some advantages to training your employees.

You can choose the training to give your staff, so, pick skills that will benefit your property. Owners should put thought into developing training programs that fit the company culture.

- *Trained employees will be better equipped to handle customer inquiries, complaints, make sales or use computer systems.*
- *You are showing your employees that you value them by investing. This increases staff retention and improves loyalty.*

- *Employees that are continually trained feel more stability in their job, become more engaged in your property and are involved in working for your success.*

- *Training is an excellent recruiting tool. You are more likely to attract and keep good employees if you can offer development opportunities.*

- *Training promotes job satisfaction. Nurturing employees to develop more rounded skill sets will help them contribute more to the property.*

- *Trained employees look for the next new challenge and will be more likely to stay if you offer them the opportunity to learn and grow while at your company. Don't give them a reason to move on by letting them stagnate once they've learnt the initial tasks.*

- *Training adds flexibility and efficiency to your employees if you cross-train them to be capable in more than one aspect of the business. This can be enormously helpful when setting schedules or filling in for absences. Cross-training is also great for your property's team spirit, as employees appreciate the challenges faced by co-workers.*

- *By spreading knowledge around among your employees, you will help save a lot of time and stress if someone suddenly leaves the property. It's like diversifying your investments.*

- *Training gives seasonal workers a reason to return. By giving seasonal employees a chance to learn new skills, you are showing them there is more than one way to contribute and saves you from having to hire and train new employees.*

- *When employees acquire new skills their self-esteem increases, and they'll be more likely to promote your property as a whole.*

- *When employees are trained, they stay fresh and motivated.*

Learning and upgrading employee skills makes good business sense. It has to start from day one and becomes successive as your employees grow.

Now, it may take some time to see a return on your investment, but the long-term gains associated with employee training make a huge difference down the road. The short-term expense of a training program ensures you keep qualified and productive workers who will help your property grow. That is a better return than you can get at most banks.

Another good reason to invest in your employees is the cost of turnover. A recent survey indicated that 40 percent of employees who receive poor job training leave their positions within the first year. They name the lack of skills training and development as the primary reason for leaving.

3.1 Consider the cost of replacing an employee

- *With one fewer worker, your property's productivity is going to slip.*
- *Your sales might decline.*
- *Your current employees have to take on extra work.*
- *Morale might suffer and to find a replacement, you spend time screening and interviewing applicants.*
- *Once you hire someone, you need to train that person.*
- *The cost of employee turnover quickly adds up.*
- *Numbers may vary, but with time and replacement costs it could reach as much as $2,500 depending on the position.*

That is a heavy price to pay for not training staff.

3.2 When is a good time to train?

- *When performance appraisal shows performance improvement is needed.*
- *As part of succession planning to help an employee be prepared for new roles at your property.*
- *When testing new systems.*
- *As part of an overall professional development program, and these could include themes such as:*

Communications

Proper communication in the workplace is a must and today with the diversity of the workforce, consideration has to be made with a wide variety of languages and customs.

This could be coupled with:

Diversity

Diversity training usually includes explanations of how people have different perspectives and views.

Computer skills

Computer skills are becoming a necessity for all aspects of the hospitality property industry.

Customer service

With competition the way it is today, customer service has to be at the top of your list, so employees must understand and meet the needs of customers.

Ethics

What is your property's social responsibility? Also, today's diverse workforce brings a wide variety of values and morals to the workplace.

Human relations

The increased stresses of today's workplace can include misunderstandings and conflict. Training can help people to get along in the workplace.

Safety

Safety training is extremely important in the workplace environment which could include methods on heavy lifting, working with chemicals, repetitive activities as well as practical advice for avoiding assaults, etc.

Sexual harassment

Sexual harassment training usually includes a careful description of the organization's policies about sexual harassment, especially about what are inappropriate behaviours. Too often, independent hotels, resorts, inns and bed and breakfast owners/managers fail to see the value in providing a formal training program.

Running on tight budgets, entrepreneurs are focused on the bottom line and think they can do the training themselves. This is where you have to think like a president and not a shareholder. For me, this is a no-brainer, training programs are a win-win for both your property and the employees. Training can also allow your employees to solve some business issues without having to go to you all the time, as well as finding new ways of generating revenue.

3.3 Developing a training program

Training can be unstructured or structured.

Unstructured is often free or low-cost programs that can involve coaching, mentoring or the new hire shadowing a more senior professional. This would be on-the-job training.

This is where an independent or smaller property has the opportunity to shine because its size allows employees to take on a variety of roles.

Structured training could be a set time.

The Internet is a good place to start.

There are many professional associations, vendors and local chambers of commerce that offer training sessions for specific industries and products. These are typically at a low cost and short duration. Guest speakers, internal YouTube videos, webinars and brown-bag lunches can also be an easy way to get started.

Pooling resources with other businesses is a way to save costs, you can have a trainer come out and do training for all the businesses together.

3.4 A couple of things to keep in mind before you get started

Most business owners think they are good leaders by default. Sorry to dissolution you but this is not always the case. Property owners should be trained as well. It is OK to admit you don't know everything.

Do assessments first. Make sure you are using your time and resources to target the areas where training is needed. Schedule a regular time for training. It doesn't have to be all the short increments.

Bottom line: Training has to be a well-thought-out priority. This is a must for the growth of your employees and your property. Now you know why you have to train, in the next chapter I will look at how to train.

4. How To Train For Success

When a hospitality property is small or independent, what is the best way to train new staff and keep them passionate about their work?

This is a good question to ask yourself.

There is always something new to learn. The day you stop learning is the day you stop living. We should all pick up new skills, ideas, viewpoints and ways of working every day. This is not a rule for your work but a rule for life.

The first goal of any property is simply to survive. To do this you need a business model that works and you always need to prove that your business model works.

To keep these excellent employees you have to help them to continue to learn and improve their skills.

This isn't an option!

If your people aren't growing in their careers as your business grows and develops, they will quickly lose enthusiasm for their work and your property. Before you know it, you will have unhappy employees as well as unhappy customers. When you have excellent employees, most often they have a desire to learn, which gives you and your business a competitive advantage over other companies.

Small properties have an opportunity to attract people who are eager to try fresh approaches and have great ideas about how to do things differently, rather than employees who are working toward attaining a specific post or title.

4.1 Your training has to be step-by-step

Have everything in writing.

Your operations manual has to have a written training manual that contains specific instructions and reference information. This will be an incredible resource for any new employee and will quicken their success.

It is the trainer's responsibility to create a safe, non-threatening environment for learning. For this to work, the trainer must have great people skills. They have to remember that new employees are people, so it is important to take the time to get to know the new members, establish a relationship, and treat them like they would like to be treated. The trainer has to plan to be patient and set a reasonable pace when teaching new tasks. A good idea is to have them think back to when they were learning something new for the first time. A hectic pace and a busy environment will only lead to problems.

Provide notebooks and pens to new employees and include in the notebook a complete description of the new employee's job, a schedule of the training process and the list of the most common questions with answers. This will help put the new tasks they are learning in context.

4.2 Before a trainer begins

Have them go through the training procedure themselves.

A good trainer will know what's expected of the employee in their new position, but they don't always know for sure if those expectations come through in the training process. The trainer going through the program and looking at it from the new employee's perspective can help. Here it is a good idea to get feedback from senior employees and make sure the common questions or concerns are covered.

From the very beginning of the training, watch the employees and ask questions to make sure things are clear.

This is very important.

Don't ever demean or talk down to a new employee. This is important for all employees. If employees are having problems understanding any aspect of the training, use relevant experiences or an example to explain or make things clear.

When you see things are starting to click, challenge them. Add on other responsibilities that you know are achievable, give them scenarios that you know can happen and see how they would respond.

In all aspects of the training, make sure to enforce that customer service as a top priority.

Be there to guide them, using your expertise, steering away from any indecisions or bad behaviours before they become a bad habit. The trainer should use current staff as experts showing how specific procedures work in the day-to-day operation.

Give praise when deserved

Yes, in a perfect world, excellence would be a matter of course, but not showing appreciation might make an employee wonder if they are living up to your expectations. You don't have to go overboard, just a *"good job"* or *"well done"* will work.
Even a smile will go a long way.

Also, criticism is important to correct bad behaviour before becomes a habit. Make sure it's constructive and with an alternative solution. Again, I can't stress enough the importance of a step-by-step procedure for all aspects of your business. With the accurate step-by-step process, owners, trainers and new staff will not be second-guessing.

4.3 Segment your training

Acquiring the knowledge to do one task at a time well, will help your employees gain confidence, and as the confidence grows, so does the desire to master the next segment.

Avoid the temptation to over talk and micromanage. Both of these tactics send the signal that you lack confidence in your employee's abilities. Quite often these tactics are enough to have good potential employees quit. These are the guidelines we recommend when training new employees, but this is just the beginning.

4.4 Here are some specifics that should be covered in the initial training.

- *A clear job description outlining their responsibilities, and the importance of their role in the bigger picture.*
- *Clarify basic standards of dress*
- *Staff behaviour*
- *Break allowance and meals*
- *Health and safety*
- *The specific products available at your property (more about this in the upselling chapter)*
- *Specify your establishment's standards for welcoming and greeting customers*
- *Dealing with their questions*
- *Dealing with difficult situation*
- *Customer complaints*
- *Awkward customers*
- *Support and teamwork*

- *Make sure the organizational structure is clear and that they know the line of reporting, and who to go to for help and guidance when needed.*
- *Contact numbers*
- *Establish procedures for sickness reporting*

Your goal is not only to have employees who can follow the step-by-step procedures for all their tasks but also to be able to think on their feet, and this means all employees on your property.

When a rule exists that has to be followed, give the reason why so it is clear, for example, safety regulations or specific laws, otherwise encourage your employees to think outside the box, especially when it comes to customer service. It has to be OK for an employee to step away from their task to help a customer with directions or to give advice on an attraction or even a little small talk. By giving them the freedom to do things with your customers, can enhance your customer's stay, you'll have a happy employee who knows how to do their job, follow the rules and bend them when necessary.

When getting to know new employees, ask them about their hobbies, their interests, about any special skills they may have.

You might have hired a housekeeper and found out that you have a blogging expert in your employee. You may have hired a maintenance person and found you have an amateur historian working with you. You might find employees with ambition and talent to help you take your business to the next level.

Encourage new employees all employees to look for ideas to make their jobs easier or to enhance your property. Have them be on the lookout for new technology opportunities that you and your employees can explore, even if you're not sure they can be immediately applied to your business. Who knows, you could be onto the next big thing and gain more of an advantage over your competition.

4.5 Here are some other training techniques to consider

Job Shadowing:

This allows an employee to learn about and benefit from the expertise of the senior employees.

Employee Interests:

If an employee has an interest in or has expertise in a subject, or attends an external training session or conference that could be of benefit to your property, have them hold an in-house training session for all employees. If there are costs involved you could offer to cost-share or pay the entire amount. This is effective employee development because it introduces new ideas to your organization.

Hold brown bag lunches:

These are informal talks about subjects over lunch. Whether about work or work-life topics, brown bag lunches can provide employees with the information they need for a better work environment and create great lives. How can this not be good for an employer?

Training from external sources:

If a company wants to sell you a new interactive computer and television system, have their sales representative come in and meet with you and your housekeeping team. As your front-line team in the rooms, they will probably be the first asked about how it works.

Making time for employee development, regularly, allows you to plan and bring in consultants or internal providers who know your goals, language, culture, and workplace norms. These job training sessions also build the team and help employees develop conversations about improvement, growth, and change.

The first six weeks are essential to any new employee; it's during this time that they decide whether or not this is the right job for them. It might be a surprise for you to hear but 33% of hospitality businesses don't do any training. If this is the case, how on earth do people know what is expected of them on a day-to-day basis, let alone know how they can contribute to the business or develop their career?

Training your staff in the basics of your property puts them in a better position to contribute to cost control and possibly generate income. If people understand how the business makes its money, they are then in a position to contribute to this and put forward their ideas. You can hedge your bet with a well-thought-out step-by-step training process and chisel a new employee into that creative, ambitious worker you so desire.

5. Effective Communication Will Improve Your Property

Communication is something we do automatically- like breathing. We have been talking since we were small; talk to our partners, kids, and friends without giving it a thought. It might seem easy, but communicating efficiently actually takes quite a bit of skill.

Choosing the right words, listening with our minds instead of just our ears, and getting our message across are skills that we all need to work on.

When at home or with friends, not finding the right words or miscommunication can lead to problems or even arguments.

At work, the results could be much worse.

Unenthusiastic employees, poor productivity, even legal issues can be the result of bad communication skills. This does not have to be a problem at your property if you incorporate a few changes to your communications practices.

Since the end of the last century, many companies have become dependent on e-mail as their primary source of communication with colleagues and outside clients.

Many of us have become so reliant on our computers and e-mail that we've neglected the art of conversation. E-mail does have its advantages over the old-fashioned *snail mail,* letters because they are quick and direct, and they do leave a trail of your correspondents, but unfortunately for many, the desire for speed has almost created a whole new language of short sentences and abbreviations.

Have you ever sent off an e-mail with the best intentions only to have that misunderstood at the other end? An e-mail sent quickly can easily be misinterpreted as a lack of caring, or worse a sign that you're mad.

When speaking to someone face to face, a conversation is more than words themselves. It's the tone of voice, facial expressions and body language.

Take body gestures and smiles out of the equation, and recipients can easily get the wrong idea, especially when the sender isn't the most coherent writer.

5.1 Ways to improve your email communication

- *When sending an e-mail, writing a letter or even a note, I use spell check, and after you have used spell check, have someone else read it. I can almost guarantee you'll find mistakes in this book, even though spell check has been used and was reread by an editor, so it's not a good idea to trust your abilities alone.*

- *Don't send messages with all caps, recipients might feel like you're YELLING!*

- *Please, please, please use complete sentences.*

- *Organize your inbox, making sure priority messages are dealt with immediately. Use folders to prioritize. Missing important emails could cost you money.*

- *Check to make sure everything is clear. A good clear message can build engagement, prevent problems and streamline efforts.*

- *Have a standard communications schedule, here you can highlight import messages. Refrain from sending an e-mail every time you have a thought. This can become overwhelming clutter and important messages will be missed.*

- *Document. Document everything and make sure it is clear. When was the last time you said or one of your employees say "Didn't I tell you?" or "Sorry, I forgot to mention" or "It's supposed to be done this way".*

It is imperative to work together as a team, and as a team you will receive the same information. Check and recheck to make sure this is happening.

5.2 Handle conflicts with tact

When you have more than two people working together 8 hours a day, day after day, week after week, month after month, year after year you're going to eventually have some issues. Minor issues will quite often take care of themselves, but those that blow into major issues can be very disruptive and stressful. In any situation like this, you want to nip it in the bud immediately.

A good start is to let all employees know from day one your door is always open. You have to create a safe environment in which employees feel comfortable, be honest, and openly voice their frustrations. Encourage them to come to you with any problems and make sure all conversations held in your office remain completely confidential. This is very important when responding to conflicts.

You have to be neutral and keep an open mind. Ask questions, and listen to the answers so you understand how each person in the dispute feels. Here, you can help the two parties reach a resolution that's acceptable to everyone. If you have a policy in place in your operations manual for this type of situation use it. If the policy is to blame, change it and if there is no policy for this issue and you feel one is justified, add it.

5.3 Respect cultural variances

Our world is getting smaller and more and more hospitality properties are hiring foreign employees as well as receiving guests from every corner of the planet. For this reason, property owners need to be more culturally sensitive and aware of the little differences in the way people of different nationalities interpret words and gestures.

I ran into this problem myself one time when in Istanbul.

A Turkish friend of mine was at one end of a busy hotel lobby, and I was at the other. He held his arm up and pointed to his watch indicating he wanted to know what time we were going to leave.

I held my hand to indicating 2 pm but instead of using the victory signal, I use the American and Canadian football signal for the second down, which was the index and pinky finger extended.

He raced across the lobby and told me to never use that signal in Turkey. It had been the sign of a past political party that had been responsible for many deaths.

On an interesting note, the V for victory sign would have been unacceptable in Australia, as that is their way of giving the finger.

It is so important to create an environment that is understanding of, and sensitive to, the needs of employees and customers, no matter what the culture or religion.

I had one property owner once tell me that if his employees or guests do not like or could not deal with his beliefs, that was their problem. Needless to say, he did not have many happy employees or a high return rate.

This is a wonderful topic to include in your training program.

5.4 Feedback is important

I have mentioned before that praise was important for your employees. Just as important as praise is feedback. If you have employees working hard for you, tell them; and if you have employees who are not pulling their weight, tell them. You don't have to hold regular meetings to share feedback, you can let employees know what you're thinking by e-mail, a phone call or the way I think works the best, in person.

When offering feedback be as clear as possible. If you're giving praise, give specific examples. Most employees enjoy hearing details when they are doing something right and if there's a problem, don't just say *"You're not finishing your tasks on time"*, offer a solution. You could say, *"There seems to be a problem with your workload, what can we do to help?"*

Talking down or being demeaning to a person is never the solution.

5.5 When to hold meetings

It is understandable that when operating a hospitality property unless closed for the season, holding staff meetings with everybody in attendance, is almost impossible.

"So what's the solution?"

A short note that every morning might work. It could state how many guests arriving; any VIPs (*very important person/ persons*) who might be on the property; any events taking place; menu specials or any product specials. I cannot emphasize this enough, unless it is an emergency or highly confidential, you should not hold a meeting with an employee in your office.

You're the face of your property, you have to be out and about as much as possible talking with your guests. So with this in mind, if you have to meet with an employee, go to where they are. This way you can share the information you need to share, watch how things are going and you're not taking that employee away from their duties. If you want to keep good open communication with your employees, make them feel like owners.

If you have utilized the proper hiring process and have incorporated step-by-step and ongoing training, then it should be obvious to your employees that you have a vested interest in them and at this point, employees should have invested interest in your property. So don't stop there.

If you have major decisions that have to been made about your property and will affect your employees, let them have a say before a decision is made. For example:

Major renovations, group insurance, policy changes for the operations manual.

Make sure you educate them on all aspects of the decision but then let them have a vote.

You might be thinking, *"Wait a minute, this is my business"* but think about it. If your employees see that you value their opinions, they will feel like they have more of a vested interest in the business and reward you with incredible loyalty. Be open with them on how business is going. If bookings are great and revenue is up, tell them. If things are slow, tell them that as well.

You might be feeling that you're giving up control when in fact, it has been proven many times, employees that who feel they have a vested interest will work harder for your success. It's all about open communication.

5.6 Emotions on the job can be a killer

Being friends with your employees is great, letting them know they can talk to you at any time is very important but what is also very important is that you're the boss. You are running a business, this is your livelihood; you have to be professional.

With any independent operation and different personalities, this can be difficult.

If an employee, for some reason is not happy and starts making negative conversations personal, there is a good chance you are going to feel irritated. This is the time to stop, take a step back, calm yourself down, don't be emotional but instead professional.

When responding, don't make it personal. Ask your employee to present their case in a clear, concise way and you listen. Don't say anything until they are finished. When they're finished, repeat their concerns to make sure it is clear. If they start to interrupt you, you can say *"I'm sorry, I thought you're finished"* and then don't say anything.

It is very difficult to argue if only one person is talking.

Once the problem is clear, offer solutions if you have them. If not, ask them what they would suggest. If you remain calm and professional, most problems will quickly find an agreeable solution.

I mentioned when listening to a complaint or a discussion it is important for you to listen. Listening, sometimes is not that easy.

To be a good listener takes practice. So how can you improve?

Challenge yourself!

Whenever you're listing to a conversation, pretend there's a test at the end and you will have to list the three most important items in that conversation. It is not as easy as you would think. With practice and little time, it will soon become second nature.

Another way to know what you heard is to repeat what the person said. This is good for both memory and clarification.

5.7 Have fun at work

Okay, you have excellent employees; they understand your business goals and objectives; they are well-trained, following all these step-by-step procedures from your operations manual and you all enjoy open and clear communications. Is that all? Even companies with the best intentions are sometimes monotonous. Is there anything else you can do to enhance the work atmosphere?

Have fun!

The workday can be as fun and as exciting as your company wants to make it. Many successful hospitality property owners that I've talked to over the years have one thing in common, they enjoy what they do not that every day is a barrel of laughs, but there is enough happiness generated over time to see them through the rough times.

5.8 How to motivate your employees

Here are some examples of things you could try:

Encourage your employees to take a few minutes every day to get out and walk around.

It has been proven that just a few minutes can energize the body and boost creativity.

Let your employees make their work environment a place they enjoy being.

For example, housekeepers keeping notes of thanks or pictures of their family or vacation in their work area. Any memento from a pleasant experience that might make them smile when they look at it.

Laugh

Yes, professionalism is very important that doesn't mean you can't smile or joke. A smile or a laugh can be contagious and when you're happy, endorphins are released, which are natural pain and stress relievers.

Compliment your co-workers every day

You'll feel just as good giving the compliment as you would receiving it.

Check-in with your colleagues
Just to say *"hi"* or drop a note to see how they're doing can brighten up everyone's day significantly.

Be appreciative
If someone is always willing to go the extra step, let them know how meaningful that is, which makes any workday better.

If you're lucky enough to find something you're good at and love doing, you're less likely to think of it as *just work.* You don't have to come up with these ideas yourself. Go online for ideas or ask your employees.

Giving employees a few minutes a day to cut loose can make them much more appreciative and productive when they do need to put their noses to the grindstone.

5.9 Guidelines for answering your properties phone

Answering your properties phone
When people call you looking for information or to get a reservation, they want to talk to a live person, not a recorded robot.

If you operate a small property and are not always at the desk to take a call, get call forwarding, answering service or extra staff if you need to. Make sure a real human is answering your business phone. The next step is to make sure the person answering your property's phone is using the appropriate skills for business. For many guests, the phone will be their first point of contact and first impression of your business.

Here's how to answer the phone properly and win business
a) Answer all incoming calls before the third ring.

b) When you answer the phone, smile, be warm and enthusiastic. Your voice on the phone can make a major impression on a possible guest.

c) When answering the phone, welcome callers courteously and identify yourself and your property. Say, for instance, *"Good morning. Twin Oaks Inn. Sandra speaking. How may I help you?"* No one should ever have to ask if they reached *"Twin Oaks Inn"*.

d) Enunciate, speaks slowly and keeping your voice volume moderate, so your caller can understand you easily.

e) Don't use buzzwords or slang or use fillers when you speak. For example, *"uh-huh"*, *"um"*, or phrases such as *"like"* or *"you know"*.

   Quite often we do not realize we're doing this, so record your voice, listen for the filler words, and to train yourself to recognize them when you are speaking. With practice, you'll soon be able to remove these filler words from your speech pattern.

f) Be positive when phone answering, even on a down day. For example, rather than saying, *"I don't know"*, say, *"Let me find out about that for you"*.

g) Take phone messages completely and accurately using full sentences. If there's something you don't understand or can't spell, such as a person's address or surname, ask the caller to repeat it or spell it for you. It is quite acceptable.

h) Return your messages within one day at the latest. I can't emphasize this one enough. Remember the early bird? That one missed call might become a long-term customer for your competition.

i) Always ask the caller if it's all right to put them on hold when answering the phone, and don't leave people on hold. Provide callers on hold with progress reports every 30 to 45 seconds. Offer them choices if possible, such as *"That line is still busy. Will you continue to hold or should I have _________ call you back?"* When on hold, don't leave your callers listening to dead air. Have soothing music playing and occasional promotions for your products.

j) Don't use a speaker phone unless necessary. The caller might feel that you are multitasking and leave the impression that you're not fully concentrating on their call.

k) If you have to use an answering machine to answer calls, make sure that you have a professional message recorded, using the same guidelines as in tip #c, and an idea of when they can expect their call returned. Make sure your answering machine message is up to date.

l) Train everyone else who answers the phone to answer the same way.

6. Enhance Your Customer Service

Excellent customer service is the lifeblood of any hospitality property.

You can extend promotions and cut room rates to bring in as many new guests as you want, but unless you can get some of those guests to come back, your property will not be lucrative for long.

Good customer service is about inviting guests in, giving them an excellent experience, sending them away happy enough to want to come back and then passing positive feedback about your property to others who may want to try it, and in turn become repeat guests. If your property looks pleasant, you may get a guest once. It is the way you deal with that person, the customer service, which will determine if that guest would want to come back. Customer service means forming a relationship with your guests, a relationship that the guest would like to continue.

How do you form such a relationship?

By remembering
"You and your property will be judged by what you do, not what you say."

This may sound simple but providing great customer service means consistency and consistency can only happen if you have a working organizational structure in place.

Is there a way to tell if your customer service is working? Do you recognize any of these?

- *Does it seem that you have had more than your fair share of complaints recently?*
- *Do your employees feel dejected and this is affecting your guests?*
- *Are you getting the initial business, but the reviews are not great and you're getting little repeat business?*
- *No one is booking even though you're offering some real enticing incentives?*

Maybe none of these is a problem, but you realize the value of delivering an excellent customer experience and it could be costly to let that slip. There are many different ways to enhance your guest's experience with great customer service. Let's take some time and I will give you an idea of what I'm talking about.

Your goal is to find employees that will benefit your property. Not everyone is cut out to work in the hospitality industry. A great hospitality property employee can be compassionate.

6.1 Empathize with your guests

A great hospitality property employee is one the guests feel is on their side. *"What other traits and skills are necessary for your hospitality property employees if you want to be able to offer consistent and great customer service?"*

1. Patience

The ability to remain calm, quiet, even temperate, and diligent when confronted with what could be considered a stressful situation. The ability to stay relaxed during tiresome situations will come across as great customer service, and great service beats fast service every time.

2. Attentiveness

The ability to listen to customers is so crucial for providing great customer service and by listening to I mean to the actual words and watching the body language. Guests might be saying one thing that means something else.

3. Clear Communication Skills

For those of you who love to talk and talk and talk, or for those of you that are mumblers, this is important. It's okay to find out more about your customers, but they don't need to know how your day is going.

When giving information make sure it is clear and concise. You do not want your guests walking outside, or going to the room, scratching their head saying *"What did they say?"*

When it comes to important points that you need to relay clearly to customers, keep it simple and leave nothing to doubt.

4. Knowledge of the Product

Make sure all your employees know all about your property and any services you may provide. If they'd don't know what you have to offer inside and out, you're leaving money on the table.

5. Able to Use "Positive Language"

Language is a very important part of influence, and guests create opinions about you and your property based on the language you use.

Small changes that utilize *positive language* can greatly affect how the customer hears your response...for example:

* Without positive language: *"Sorry, there are no reservations available in the restaurant at 8:00 pm."*

* With positive language: *"You have a choice, you can enjoy a pre-dinner drink in our bar and dine at 9:00 PM or dine at 7:00 PM and then enjoy an after-dinner stroll on our grounds."*

6. Acting Skills

This is a skill that every great hospitality property employee needs. There are going to be people that you come across, that will not be happy no matter what you do. Here you have to fake it.

7. Time Management Skills

If you're dealing with two situations at the same time, or a situation where you do not know the answer, find the best person available to help you. Don't waste time trying to go above and beyond for a customer in an area where you will just end up wasting both of your time!

8. Ability to "Read" Customers

You won't always be able to see customers face-to-face, and in many instances, you won't even hear a customer's voice! Look and listen for subtle clues about their current mood, patience level, and personality. This can go far in keeping your customer interactions positive.

9. A Calming Presence

This is the ability to stay calm and even influence others when things get a little hectic. The best hospitality property employees know that they cannot let a heated customer force them to lose their cool; in fact, it is their job to try to be the *rock* for a customer who thinks the world is falling due to their current problem.

10. Ability to Handle Surprises

It is in these situations when it is best for you or an employee to be able to think on your feet... but it's even better to create guidelines for yourself in these sorts of situations. If a well-trained employee is faced with a situation that surprises them, and they handle it the best way they see fit, you have to be willing to support them in their decision.

11. Persuasion Skills

If you have a property that offers additional services or products, being able to upsell is a skill that can be beneficial to both your employees and your business. I discuss this further later.

12. Resolve

A great work ethic and a willingness to do what needs to be done is a key skill when providing the kind of service that people talk about.

The many memorable customer service stories out there were created by a single employee who refused to just do the *status quo* when it came to helping someone out.

13. Willingness to Learn!

This is probably the most general skill on the list, but it's still necessary. If you're following the guidelines I have shared so far, this is a skill that you defiantly have.

6.2 Ways to surprise guests & not spend a fortune

Something I have noticed over the years is that it is the little things that people remember. One way to surprise your guests is by doing a little research. When taking the reservation, whether it be online or over the phone, you should have a question or space for special occasions.

For example, when taking a phone reservation and it's for the weekend, you could say *"The weekends here are wonderful, great for special getaways"*.

This is a type of leading sentence and the guest might give you the reason for the booking. If the guest mentions the booking is for a wedding anniversary or a birthday, you could leave a box of chocolates in the room the day they arrive. This question or one similar should be part of a standard script when taking reservations but made to sound like part of the conversation.

I've mentioned this story before. Once my wife and I visited a bed & breakfast in a vineyard in Germany.

The hosts invited us down for a glass of wine and when we were finished, gave us the glasses. The glasses were etched with the logo of the winery.

The glasses were beautiful and I asked the host about the price, and he told me they were was less than two euros each because of bulk buying, and then he said, *"Of course, we price that into the cost of the room"*.

We keep the glasses prominently displayed and quite often they're a topic of conversation.

We've been back many times and consider the owner's friends.

The following are some other ideas we have seen.

- Handwritten notes left on a pillow saying *"Have sweet dreams"* and *"Have a pleasant sleep"*.
- Take home puzzles of the property left in rooms of families with children.
- An owner of a property in Cape Breton, Canada, caters to an older clientele and always asks when they arrive if for any reason they would like to visit a drugstore to let her know, and they will be driven. Very few take advantage but everybody remembers.

- One property I stayed at was so proud of the cleanliness of their rooms, they challenged you to find dirt. Under the bed was a card that said that *"yes we clean here, and for finding the card come to the desk for a free specialty coffee"*.
- I was travelling with a group in Newfoundland and Labrador, Canada and when we checked in, the front-desk employee offered each of us a small plate of a local fish speciality, cod cheeks & tongue. This is something that I probably would not have chosen from a local menu, but they were delicious! This happened 20 years ago and it's still a great memory.
- After a week on the road in Ireland, my wife and I checked in to a bed & breakfast in Galway. We had laundry to be done and ask the owner for the closest Laundromat we could take our wash. She said *"you'll do no such thing"*, took our wash and told us to go enjoy the sights. When we arrive back the wash was done and neatly folded in our room.

These were little extras that would not have been missed if not done, but have since become memories and stories to be shared.

If at all possible, when a guest checks out, do not let them leave empty-handed.

These are items that should not be expensive but are tangible such as:
- *A coffee mug and cover with the property logo, filled with coffee.*
- *A reusable water bottle with the property logo.*
- *As I mentioned before, the wine glasses*

- *A small book with the history of your property or region*
- *Your house speciality or local recipe*
- *Tea canister*
- *The small framed picture of the property or region*
- *Something in the region is known for i.e. chocolate, jams, or fruit*

The ideas are endless. Remember, your goal is to stand out from your competitors.

7. How To Handle Customer Complaints

With the continued evolution of online hotel, resort, inn and bed & breakfast review sites, social media, forums, and fuming customers on YouTube, a property's level of guest service is increasingly visible to the outside world. For this reason, you must have a working operation manual with the appropriate policies to handle customer complaints, as well as the properly trained staff who not only welcome guest complaints but actually, encourage them. Unfortunately, many hospitality property employees believe the handling of complaints is an unlikeable task but one that comes with the job.

With proper policies in place and training from day one on how to use these policies, employees can change their view of customer complaints. Employees and especially owners of independent hotels, resorts, inns or bed & breakfasts should look at customer complaints as an opportunity.

"The worst complaints are the ones you do not hear."

The majority of guests who were not happy with your property did not voice their opinion to the owner or the front desk but instead told their friends, family and colleagues and in more and more cases went online to express their irritation. Yes, some customers do complain, thus offering you a chance to find a solution, but what about all those customers who do not say anything. This is where training should involve employees to look for unhappy customers and allow them to complain.

I have an example, not from the hospitality property but a restaurant, a very well-known restaurant, on the waterfront in Halifax, Nova Scotia, Canada.

Over the years, I had recommended this restaurant to many people and one day, while eating there, the owner came over to me and said: *"Gerry, you send many people our way, do you ever get negative feedback?"*

I said, *"No, I don't, why do you ask?"*

He said *"I know our restaurant has a great reputation but I also know we cannot do everything right all the time and if I don't know there's a problem, it's very difficult to fix. If you ever get any complaints, please let me know".*

This is a restaurant, but the same applies to hotels, resorts, inns and bed & breakfasts.

Most people are not comfortable with the idea of being confrontational and would much prefer leaving a property, not saying anything, but never returning.

So, how can you get a customer, a guest, who was not happy with something to tell you? There are a couple of ways I have seen work.

Have a specific e-mail address on the bill, on the evaluation form and in the room's information packet for complaints.

For example, _complaints@myproperty.com_

I've also seen the same idea with a specific telephone number — a complaint hotline.

The best way is to have employees who can read a guest. This is done with proper training. If the guest is in front of you, with training and practice you can tell if a guest is unhappy by listening to their voice, watching their facial expressions or body language. If the guests on the phone, listen to the tone of voice. Here you have an opportunity to be proactive and by asking the right questions a guest might tell you their concerns.

I have seen many cases, where an employee might sense there's a problem but will purposely avoid asking for any feedback to avert a confrontation. An employee with the right training and attitude will avoid any kind of confrontation by asking the right questions.

Questions you should stay away from are the ones where one-word answers can be given, like *"How was your stay?"* or *"Did you have a good night?"*

Instead, you want to ask questions that require more thought and response. For example *"We're very interested in what you thought of our property?"* or *"Is there anything we could have done to make your visit more enjoyable?"*

Train your employees to look into your guest's eyes with sincerity and genuine interest in their response.

When asking questions like these, employees are encouraging your guest to give honest feedback and to maybe tell you about any problems. By being proactive, and embracing complaints instead of ignoring them, hospitality properties have an opportunity to solve a complaint and turn an unhappy guest into a pleased guest, especially if they are happy with the way the complaint is resolved.

You may be thinking, *"This might be a little easier said than done"*.

You're right, training your employees to invite negativity might seem like an uphill battle, so let's look at a couple of ways to applaud guest complaints.

- Have a bell or buzzer to ring in the back office when a complaint is received. Train everyone to feel that when the buzzer rings, there is an opportunity to turn a problem around.

- Track the complaints and measure monthly. Have the employees document the name of the guest, their room number, the complaint, the action is taken and whether the guest was happy with the outcome. As time goes on, and problems are rectified, the number of complaints should decrease. These forms can be used as training tools, ways to handle better similar complaints in the future.

7.1 Here some tips for employees to use

- The first one is a skill or a trait every good employee should have; the ability to listen without speaking. Let the guest explain their complaint. Quite often this venting will take the form of a detailed story.

- Maintain eye contact, demonstrating concern but remain quiet. If you're taking the complaint on the phone, don't respond until the complaint is finished but it is OK to interject the occasional *"alright"*, *"I see,"* and *"okay"*
.

- When the guest is finished telling their story, show compassion and give an apology. The apology does not mean you're wrong or is an admission of guilt, it just means you understand your guest's displeasure. You could say *"I understand how you must feel; I can imagine I might feel the same way given the circumstance"*. The words *"feel"* and *"imagine"* are powerful in these cases.

- Re-state their complaint in a condensed version to show you understand the situation and provide validation for the guest. *"Mr. Richter, I understand your frustration. You're tired and hungry and room service is this slow." Again, it is OK to say "I'm sorry".* You might be surprised to hear that more often than not, guest service employees never offer an apology or worse an insincere apology.

- When guests complain, they want results.

In a perfect world, you could give them what they want, but we are in the real hospitality property world, and that is not always possible. A great way to handle the guest's complaint is to offer them two options. By being offered two options, they are allowed to make a choice, which will feel empowering.

Trained staff who are proactive, can find unhappy guests, uncover a problem, and help properly resolve it can reduce the odds of further complaints and online rants. By being understanding and helpful you can turn a disgruntled guest into a loyal patron who might be happy to share the news about your great service. Independent hotels resorts, inns and bed & breakfasts are in the business of customer satisfaction.

"The customer is not always right, but it is your job to make them think they are."

I don't feel that in the immediate future all hospitality properties will be operated by robots, so for the foreseeable future, there is a good chance that human error will still be the source of problems at properties.

7.2 The most common problem's hospitality properties have

1.   Room cleanliness

At a minimum, rooms must meet basic hygienic standards. This can be accomplished with a complete checklist followed daily.

2.   Poor room service

If you offer room service, make sure you have the staff to handle it.

3.   Restaurant food quality

I was told once by a restaurant inspector, that the first two things he looks for at a restaurant are the cleanliness of the toilet and the freshness of the lettuce. If either of these two things is a problem, there's a very good chance food quality is substandard.

4.   Laundry

If you offer laundry services for guests and a garment is damaged, make sure to bring it to their attention immediately and provide restitution. If your property provides your guests with the use of washing machines and dryers, they have to be working.

5.   Noisy rooms

If you have a room or rooms that are noisy due to traffic, construction or an elevator, make your guests aware when giving them the key. If you have this problem, have earplugs in stock.

6.   Parking

If you provide parking facilities for guests and charge them for it, make sure it is monitored.

7.   Pay-per-view Television

This can be an excellent source of revenue, but whenever a guest complains about the charge, deleted without question. It is not worth the hassle.

8.   Mini-Bar

This can also be a great source of revenue and a nuisance at the same time. If a customer complains about the charge, take them at their word. Of course, there will be those who will take advantage but look at this as the cost of doing business.

9.   Hidden charges

This is a complaint I have heard quite often. Make sure all charges are itemized on a bill. If a customer complains, do not accuse them of being wrong but instead say *"We will be happy to look into this for you"*. If you find there is a mistake, delete it immediately. If not, explain the charges to the guest.

10.   Overbooking

If you are overbooked and have to move guests to another property, make sure you have not charged them for anything, make the arrangements and pay for any transfer.

7.3 How To Handle Negative Hospitality Property Reviews

Not long ago, almost 3000 respondents were surveyed about the importance of a hospitality property responding to online reviews. These were user review online companies such as *TripAdvisor* and *booking.com.* They showed that 85% of users agree that an appropriate management response to a bad review improved their impression of the property. 64% of users agreed that an aggressive or defensive management response to a bad review made them less likely to book that property.

Bad reviews about your property can have a major negative impact on your business, so you must respond to them. By doing so you can minimize the harm to your property's reputation by making potential guests think more highly of you, and it can repair your relationship with the unhappy reviewer. It also shows potential guests that you take your reviews seriously.

Here are a couple of things to keep in mind.

- *Always research the complaint before you respond*
- *Never respond angrily*
- *Did the guest complain before checkout?*
- *Is there a record of this complaint with your staff?*

7.4 A few more points to consider

1. *Thank the guest by name*
Even if the review is nasty, using the guest's name shows you're taking this seriously.

2. *Apologize for the guest's poor experience*
Remember, an apology is not an admission of guilt or wrongdoing. Compassion can go a long way.

3. *Tell them the changes you have made or going to make*
You can do this by inviting them to phone or email you, thus taking the discussion offline. Don't ever promise any form of compensation online to avoid setting a precedent or to make it look like a payoff.

4.   *Follow up with the guest*

Send them a personal email or note, again apologizing and offering compensation if appropriate.

7.5 How to handle negative reviews on social media

You hopefully understand the importance of social media for marketing purposes. Social media can attract new customers while helping you retain the loyalty of past guests. It allows your guests to communicate with you directly, praise you for an excellent experience, or give you positive feedback, but it can also be a method for guests to share a negative experience.

> *"One bad review on Twitter or Facebook can be on tens of thousands of other timelines within a couple of days."*

Social media is a powerful marketing tool, so you have to know how to handle negative feedback, positively.

7.6 Here are a few tips

Be Responsive

If a guest leaves negative feedback, respond to it quickly to address their concerns.

The owner should approach the customer directly and with compassion, and politely ask the guest to call (toll-free number) or email you directly.

This will show:

- *That you're taking their complaint seriously and wish to try to help.*
- *You're willing to take the time to discuss this complaint personally, out of the public forum.*
- *If the guest is not willing to discuss the complaint personally, it shows other readers that you were trying to resolve their problem.*

Provide a Solution

When addressing guest complaints via social media, be concise, constructive, and clear and avoid confrontation when trying to provide a solution. Even if you know the complaint is not valid, tell them you're going to check into it and you are taking their feedback seriously. You want the guest to feel confident knowing you're working with them, rather than against them.

Keep Your Promise

If you promise a guest that gave you a bad review you're going to make things better by *(improving room service, cleaner bathrooms, friendlier service, etc.)* you had better do it. The guest who complained might not come back to check, but new guests who read the reviews and responses will expect these changes have been made. This goes toward your credibility and future profits.

Keeping all your guests happy, all the time could be hard work and tiresome, but having policies in place and training employees to use them, will save you and your employees a lot of grief. It could be fun and very rewarding.

8. How To Upsell

8.1 Why should you want to upsell?

Upselling will make your guests more satisfied and make your business more profitable.

A properly trained employee can add apparent value to a room sale that the customer is already willing to make, increasing their stay's worth as well as increasing your bottom line. This benefits everyone.

I've heard many employees and owners say they feel uncomfortable trying to upsell, like upsell or cross-sell our dirty words. Upselling doesn't have to be a dirty word. It can help you make your customers happier.

First of all, I should explain the difference between upselling and cross-selling.

Upselling is a strategy to sell a more expensive version of something the customer already has. For example, going from a standard room to a mini-suite.

Cross-selling is a strategy to sell products that are different but possibly related. For example, if your property has a swimming pool you might offer your guests swimming goggles or swimming caps.

8.2 Upsell & cross-selling are not dirty words

If done correctly, upselling can build a deeper relationship with your guests by helping your guests win. What I mean is, if you can make your customer feel like an upsell is a win for them, you both can win.

For example, a couple is checking into your property and your front desk employee says, *"Would you like me to make a dinner reservation in our restaurant? With your room rate, you qualify for our dinner special, saving you $20.00 off the normal price".*

Quite often, guests will hear they're saving $20.00 and jump at the opportunity. This is a win for the guests who are saving $20.00 and for you as they might not have taken advantage of your restaurant.

It is easier to upsell to returning guests than to new guests.

According to the book *Marketing Metrics,* the probability of selling to a new guest is 5-20%. The probability of selling to an existing guest is 60-70%. With returning guests, there is a trust factor and for that reason, upselling is easier.

Upselling increases your guest's lifetime value. Each upsell can increase the lifetime value of your loyal guests, paying off for many years down the line.

When was the last time you went into a McDonald's' and not been offered fries or a drink to go with your burger or last time you bought an electrical appliance and not been told the benefits of an extended warranty?

Maybe now you can see the benefit of learning and then teaching your employees to upsell. It is a vital skill that you can learn by approaching each sale smartly, making use of various upsell techniques, and laying the groundwork for repeat business.

8.3 What are the mechanics of upselling?

- *You need the right questions to identify the customer's wants.*
- *You need to know how to listen to the customer's preferences or requests*
- *How to answer and make suggestions or give options that meet the customer's needs.*
- *You need to know how to describe the products, services or options.*

It is not only the front desk employees or reservations that can upsell, but your housekeepers and wait staff might have an opportunity to mention products, services or options in passing.

Let all employees try or experience what you have to offer. The more they know about what you have to offer and being able to share their experiences, will add value to the offer and easier to upsell.

I highly recommend you create a script with all the details and give it to your employees, but let them develop their pitch. If it sounds more natural, it will sound more genuine. Everyone should practice their pitches on each other. Practice makes perfect.

8.4 Read your customer

If a couple is getting away for the weekend, you could offer *"couple spa treatments"* or *"candlelight dinner"*.

If it's a family, you could offer them *"a family package to the zoo"* or *"passes to the local swimming pool"*. You can set these kinds of opportunities up by cross-promoting with other businesses.

If your business includes group travel, your salesperson could offer *"baggage service"* or *"group dinner"*.

8.5 Plan for objections

It is important to train your staff to see and handle different situations. Is the objection real or just a guest's way of saying, I need more time or information?

Here are examples of situations they could come across:

- *The guest would like something but not what you offered*
- *Maybe the timing is wrong*
- *They are new to your property and you have not built trust yet*
- *They don't understand the offer*
- *Staff have to decide whether a no is a no, or request for more information*

Talk with your employees about times they were upsold, and the strategies used. Script out objections you have received for your particular offers, how they're handled and then discuss how they could be handled better.

Two great rules to follow
- *Never sell to an extremely frustrated or angry customer.*
- *Always show compassion and understanding for your guest's perspective*

8.6 Give incentives

Whether it be a small percentage of the upsell to the salesperson or an incentive that is equitable so everyone is motivated to contribute. You must give regular updates on progress. A combination of both works well. These have to be measurable goals and monitored regularly. The incentives do not always have to be financial; for example, they could be vouchers, certificates, meals or movie passes.

8.7 Guide and support

I have stressed many times in the past how important training is and when it comes to upselling, don't assume because you've told people how to do something they will be able to just go out and deliver it consistently. You have to observe how your staff handle the upselling conversation and give them feedback and because it's mutually beneficial, have employees critique and share ideas. All feedback should be positive with options.

8.8 What to promote

To do this effectively, the first thing is to determine which are the products or services you wish to promote. Whenever and whatever you decide to promote unless it is perceived as a value to the customer, you'll be wasting your time and not building customer loyalty.

The type of options I have seen work:

- *Room upgrades*
- *Special packages (if possible, utilize outside attractions and special events, as well as in house offers)*
- *Champagne, wine, chocolate and fruit in the rooms*
- *Spa or wellness treatments*
- *Outdoor excursions and attractions*
- *Theatre*

8.9 Do your guests a favour

It is a wonderful feeling when your guests rebook because they were being made to feel special. If your customer perceives what you're doing as a favour, they're much more likely to return to the place where they're treated right. One of the best ways to do your customer a favour is to navigate them toward a cheaper, but not the cheapest option.

There's nothing more convincing than lowering your voice and saying, *"Now, I probably shouldn't tell you this, but this option is (overpriced, not as much fun, not as tasty). This other option gets you the same features and you're sacrificing none of the quality, but that's my opinion, but this is what I use"*.

8.10 Be yourself

It does not matter if you are an extrovert or introvert, studies show that the best salespeople are versatile, those who can feel legitimate excitement and enthusiasm for guest's purchases. Be genuine and be honest, and you'll consistently be able to upsell.

9. How To Fire An Employee

If you're an independent hotel, resort, inn or bed and breakfast owner or manager and you're having a problem with an employee, you have two choices:

You can try to work with them, and help them improve their performance or, fire them.

Firing someone is not a decision you can take lightly. The cost of turning over an employee can be high; it could cause your employee emotional and financial stress; it could cause distress with your other employees; depending on what country are in, it could open you up to lawsuits, but unfortunately, there are times when this is your only option.

Let's look at ways to fire someone professionally, gracefully and safely.

9.1 Before you fire someone

As soon as you know there's a problem, act quickly. Sit down with your employee and discuss the problem. Ask them what they think is the cause and if possible offer suggestions for improvement.

- *Make sure you tell your employee about your concerns and that it could be grounds for termination.*
- *If it is a problem with the procedure, remind them that they accept that these terms when they were hired or when the changes were made.*
- *Give them a warning if their work is being affected due to continually missing work or insubordination.*

I have seen both property owners and managers that evaluate their employees once a year and some that never evaluate their employees. I recommend you make it a practice to talk to each of your employees at least every couple of months about their performance, how they feel about their job and how things could improve. During these meetings, you should talk about your concerns. While it is your business, you have to consider your bottom line and the effect an unproductive employee would have on the rest of your staff, you should also consider their situation.

If they have lost focus due to outside factors such as health concerns, relationship problems, divorce, death in the family, or financial problems, these are all issues that may be temporary and by everybody pulling together, you could save the loss of a valuable employee. This might allow the employee to resolve their problems and improve their performance in a timelier manner.

Make sure to have a policy in your operations manual explaining grounds for termination and go over it with the employee.

Document your conversations, and then both you and your employee sign the document or send them an e-mail with a record of the conversation and have them reply that they have read it. It is very important to keep a paper trail as well as a record of all disciplinary actions.

Give them a plan of action, specific improvements or changes required for them to keep their job, and clear deadlines of when these improvements or changes must be seen.

Set up a timeline. Not all problems can be solved as fast as we would like, but a timeline and goals with deadlines will help you see if there's any improvement, or not. If improvement is not shown, make it clear to the employee that termination is the next step.

9.2 Make a plan

Think about your employee's responsibilities and who you might reassign them to or if you have to hire a new employee. *(Be careful if you are planning to hire a new employee. If the employee you are thinking of firing sees the writing on the wall, they might start looking for a new job or if they find their job description for your company posted, they might take offence or worse, retaliatory measures.)*

If you feel the employee might fight the firing, think about offering a couple of weeks or month's pay in exchange for them signing a severance agreement.

When the time comes to fire your employee, do it privately in a place where both you and the employee can speak comfortably. There might be items that have to be discussed that need not be shared openly. Get to the point immediately, actually, it's a good idea to practice what you're going to say before the meeting.

If you have followed all the steps leading to this meeting, the employee should not be surprised and you do not have to go over the whole thing again. Just say *"I'm sorry things have not changed, I'm going to have to let you go."*

You should have written a document of the next steps and then go over it verbally. Items you might cover could include: emptying their workspace and returning any property, supplies, or equipment. Explaining the severance package, if applicable. In most cases, the person you just let go or fired is not bad, just was not suited for the job. You may offer to give them a reference regarding their reliability, their attitude, their teamwork, whatever parts of the job they were successful with.

Thank them for the work they performed well, and wish them luck in their future endeavours. If you have followed the steps, your ex-employee should not be surprised and hopefully, the parting of the ways will be cordial. Just in case, be ready in case they get upset.

If they start lashing out emotionally or get insulting, do the same as you would do with an angry guest, don't respond. Sure that might not be fair to you, but it might be what they need to get through this situation.

If for some reason they get violent, don't hesitate, call for help and police if needed.

9.3 Stay professional

It is hard to fire someone, especially if you know they need the job but you have to remember, this is your business and you're responsible for your guests and your other employees.

Alright, this is the end of the last chapter of the employee development series. I encourage you to review the information from all the chapters.

Now you know how to find, hire and train your employees, what's your next step?

You have to attract your ideal guests to your property.

Pick up the *"Marketing Strategy for Hospitality Property's"* book.

What's Next …

Operating a Successful Hospitality Property
Just Got Easier…

You're just a heartbeat away from the crucial training, advice & support you need to plan, create & grow a prosperous and rewarding, hotel, resort, inn, bed and breakfast or vacation rental.

Does any of this sound familiar?

- *You have a great idea for a hospitality property, but don't know where to start and how to turn that into a real plan...*

- *You've spent countless hours working your business but your organizational structure is lacking and you're tired of having to do everything yourself...*

- *Your employees are not living up to your standards and the good ones leave...*

- *Your marketing is not working as it should and you're not reaching your target audience…*

- *You feel you're a step or two behind your competition…*

If any of these things ring true, then you already know what a minefield it can be trying to get quality advice & support.

Introducing the Hospitality Property School Group

We are travel authorities that have spent 1000's nights in properties of all classes worldwide, conducting countless site inspections for several world-class tour companies, as well as received feedback from 100,000's of guests.

This knowledge has given us a unique insight into the wants, needs and requirements of individual and group travellers, as well as management and employees.

We provide strategies for, and aid in the growth and development of hotels, resorts, inns and bed & breakfasts to create their brand and goals; as well as increase their bookings and profit while keeping their integrity.

The Hospitality Property School Group is packed with in-depth, practical training and resources on all aspects of planning, building, running and growing a successful hospitality property.

Here is How You Will Benefit:

Actionable Workbooks

Actionable workshops are a series of short mini-courses that you can study and then utilize the best practices for your business.

Courses

The design of the courses is the result of decades of experience that have given us insight into the wants, needs & requirements of hospitality property guests, management & employees.

Resources/Perks

You have access to the free resources download centre designed to help streamline your organizational structure, grow your bookings & increase your bottom line. As a member, you deserve a break. Keystone HPD has created a number of training tutorials, ebooks, audiobooks & video production opportunities and you can SAVE up to 50%.

Member Properties

What makes your property special? Tell us about your property, your region, your success stories, your great employees, your favourite guests. Every month we'll pick our one to highlight on the group site.

Q & As

Do you have a question? Ask them here and let the experts in our community share their thoughts, tell their stories & best practices. In this section, we'll catalogue the best responses.

Community Voice

Have you had any game-changing ideas? Tell us in the "Community Voice" section and we'll share the ones we like here and in the monthly update.

You'll Also Find Material on The Following Topics:

- Your Guests
- Personal/Employee Development
- Facility
- Marketing
- Hospitality Property Checklists
- Trends
- Technology
- Operations Manual Development
- Interviews
- Webinars
- Ted Talks
- *INN*sider Tips
- Podcasts

The Hospitality Property School Podcasts provide strategies & techniques to aid in the growth & development of hospitality properties while increasing patronage & profit.

Within the group, you'll have the opportunity to ask questions, share best practices, promote your property etc.

Plus, be able to watch the training tutorials, the video podcasts and listen to the interviews when it fits into **your** schedule.

This is your group and we want you to benefit to the fullest.

WHAT MAKES THE HOSPITALITY PROPERTY SCHOOL GROUP SPECIAL?

ACCESS TO EXPERTISE
Tap into our decades of experience in the industry.

..NO B.S. ALLOWED

We're not into overblown hype, marketing tricks or jumping on the latest shiny bandwagon. Just straight-talking, honest, proven and practical advice. No B.S. or tricks!

..OUR FULL COMMITMENT

We eat, sleep and breathe the hospitality property industry. The group is our main focus and we love helping our group members achieve success. It's what we do, and we're not going anywhere!

.

Are you ready to take your property to the next level?

.

Get Instant Access to the Hospitality Property School Group!

https://member.keystonehpd.com

In case you were wondering, we have a

14 Day No Questions Asked Money-Back Guarantee

When you join the Hospitality Property School Group, you are fully protected by our 100% Satisfaction Guarantee. If you don't feel like you've received value and you decide you want to cancel any time within the next 14 days, just let us know and we'll send you a prompt refund. No hassles, headaches or hoops to jump through. We're confident that you'll find the Membership Academy useful, and we won't make you beg or invoke any silly rules or conditions - if you're not satisfied within your first 14 days then we'll refund you without any fuss.

Simply copy & click the link for your payment option to join

https://member.keystonehpd.com